DIFFICULT ARGUMENTS & SIMPLE TRUTHS

WHEN MODERN DAY AFFLICTIONS ADVANCE EXPOSURES

The strength of what we believe is measured by how much we are willing to suffer those beliefs.

TERRANCE B. MCGEE

Difficult Arguments & Simple Truths
© 2022 Terrance B. McGee

Paperback ISBN: 978-1-66786-146-3
eBook ISBN: 978-1-66786-147-0

CONTENTS

ACKNOWLEDGEMENTS

To family and friends: your strong arm of admiration and expectancy helps me to strive toward a successful journey. The confidence you bestow upon me helps to promote self-assurance and the intestinal fortitude to remain resilient in my efforts. And, because I understand the significance of a great role model, I accept my role in good faith.

PREFACE

As human beings who inhabit planet earth, we exist as breed that dwell and occupy a portion of the universe. Within our sector, we populate different regions of the world sharing some commonality amid distinct variations that constitute our differences: *gender, ethnicity* and *belief.* All three facets are susceptible to individualization. And, because we are curious about our existence, we cling and holdfast to learned traditions that which makes sense to us.

As we surface in life and are faced with daily complexities, eventually, and at some point, we question Universal Intelligence. The most obvious inquiry concerns whether there is proof.

Habitual despair can be the difference of how one day goes.

Naturally as people, we are accustomed to seeing things before trusting that something unseen to be true. As we look around us and witness this enormous reality, why is it difficult for us to believe there is a maker of our being? Since we proclaim to be a measure of Divine nature, metaphysical concepts of divine truth help us to choose how we perceive and think about things.

It has been my experience to learn and know that humans only complicate matters. We can only attempt to explain phenomena.

Although every life has its own share of tensions and dilemmas, psychological reasonings are inadequate responses against fear, doubt, temptation, and anxiety. Yet, we are not alone. Through cosmic penetration of human experiences, we gain knowledge of wisdom from that which is considered spirituality.

I find happiness to be a trained response. Any questions that our minds can conjure up or argue about, we only need to deepen our connection with Universal Intelligence to allow transformation from a self-conscious state to a humbling consciousness. Indication in life is that there will be many preachers and teachers, but none who could help us understand the divine plan for us, more than seeking and indulging for the self.

If you are someone who has not come to a firm decision on the authority of Universal Intelligence, I invite you on a journey with the hope that spiritual counsel will speak to your heart as it speaks to mine.

With every argument, there is a simple truth. Letting go of expectations, releasing attachments, silencing our egos, and facing uncertainty with faith provides assurance for that we have no control over. And because we are one through each other, being of service is the most effective way of personal study and application. Adhering to those methodologies, we might find most pleasing a simple truth and basic practice for living.

Before we begin our journey, I recommend that your quest for truth be identified with that which is pure and justifiable. Many people will sound convincing in their opinions, but we must utilize any wise discernment of Universal Intelligence to loyal our commitment.

Afflictions will occur. It is essential to communicate and seek guidance from the Celestial and most wise, for ignorance is blessed through supplication; only then is the significance of knowledge obtained free in mind.

By virtue of any thesaurus, the word "Truth" itself is substantially based upon assertion, signifying that there may be two types: Temporal (worldly) & Eternal (everlasting).

Temporal truths may be regarded as things that can be observed from a physical spectrum. Temporal truths depend upon physical revelations for validation. Thus, these disclosures have limitations, and can be altered for society appeal. Temporal truths are pragmatic approaches or rather scientific analysis that reveals partial proofs but confirms phenomena.

Revelations render divine attributes of human virtues. Therefore, man without Universal Intelligence lack reality and shows him to be separate from his ordained life. Whatever truth man has in himself is not that of truth in Universal Intelligence. And, although mysticism gives way to the embodiment of truth, spiritual certainties of those who believe receive a genuine reality, a truth that reveals something much greater than themselves.

I. ALPHA BEING

Difficult Argument: Does God exist?

Simple Truth: People are destroyed for lack of knowledge because they reject knowledge. *"Faith is the substance of things hoped for, the evidence of things not seen." Hebrews 11:1*

As difficult as the concept of origin is to grasp, we cannot dismiss the idea due to a lack of comprehension. Since we cannot phantom the derivation of things, we tend to label them for identification purposes, or to falsely acclaim as our own.

How reasonable is it that we should expect to understand all of the ways of the Celestial? Our minds cannot grasp the depth of Universal Intelligence more than an infant can understand all the ways of a parent. Besides, contributing our faith in a miraculous conception, we can hardly believe in divine intervention.

While studying biblical history, it speaks primarily about the uniqueness of God's wisdom and mercy, and suggests there are aspects of

Universal Intelligence that are too deep for our minds to fathom. The concept of God being without a beginning is apparently one of them.

Although abstract ideas can be difficult to comprehend, it is quite confusing when people say, "I hope," or "I pray," unless we believe that someone or something will provide that we are asking. Shouldn't we consider that with whom our faith resides? Without faith in something there is no hope, period.

The issue of being naive is that those who operate subconsciously, seeking to dismiss the idea of Universal Intelligence, thirst for help in times of necessity. The consequential afflictions remind us that we are helpless creatures in need of Divine intervention to help set our thinking straight.

Theoretically speaking, there could a number of reasons why someone would reject the idea of God's existence, for the challenges of life, at times, can be excruciating and viewed from a negative stance.

Positive perspectives are thought to be an understanding of righteous principles. Negative perspectives are formed by lack of knowledge, free from that of good endeavors, which perpetuate self-consciousness thereby rejecting superior guidance.

We must trust and accept that our lives are not predicated upon self-gratification, and that Universal Intelligence vision for our lives is greater than the plans that we have for ourselves.

* * *

Positive perspectives are thought to be an understanding of righteous principles. Negative perspectives are formed by lack of knowledge of good endeavors, and perpetuate self-consciousness thereby rejecting superior guidance.

* * *

Considering the foundation of God's foretold universal history, a multitude of inhabitants, both ancient and of modern generations, have written volumes of material on one man. In such a history, we can do nothing except capture a glimpse of this world and reference great nations which has risen and fallen. Yet, we're able to witness the richness and beauty of nature. We're able to witness spirituality flourishing in the lives of people. We're able to recognize elegance bestowed upon us. Without Divine counsel, we couldn't last another day and would destroy humanity based upon ungodly practices.

Are we not witnessing signs of destruction happening around the world today? How dare we ignore counsel that promotes our well-being? For, "The strength of what we believe is measured by how much we are willing to suffer those beliefs." – Terrance McGee

In September 2011, Atheists lost suit against the U.S. Treasure Department and other government officials to have "In God We Trust" phrase removed from U.S. currency. The posing argument brought forth by the Freedom of Religion Foundation was that they were "forced to proselytize – by an Act of Congress – for a deity they don't believe in whenever they handle money." The plaintiff's argued that placement of the motto on bills and coins are unconstitutional, in violation of the established clause of the First Amendment. To continue, the atheists felt that the phrase hold religious connotations that are discriminatory against non-believers.

After dismissal of the suit by U.S. Supreme Court, the case was terminated because the federal appeals court found no constitutional violation in the phrase, nor did the placement of the phrase constitute a substantial burden on atheists.

Nowadays, it seems, unconventional pursuers attempt to have any sacred connotations removed from every platform. It doesn't deem logical to have disputes against principles of unconditional love. Furthermore, what does this say about individual(s) who oppose such values?

According to biblical prophecy, people weren't excluded based upon gender or nationality, simply because these are distinctions outside of human control. Therefore, marginalized people are no different from you or me. Despite our behavior misfortunes, scarcity is imposed by those of us who are considered self-centered and greedy patrons with lack of consideration for others. Furthermore, narcissistic behavior may very well be a root cause of incredible disproportions.

Universal Intelligence suggests that divinity resides in a spiritual realm. Although it is thought to be that heaven manifest this glory, God cannot be authenticated in a physical sense. We must find a medium to reach God in a spiritual sense.

In addition, that begs the question of mind, body and soul. The mind sole intent is to possess psychological sensitivities so that we may be able to think, reason and decide. The body relates to tangible physicality's, which allows us to feel. The soul (spirit), particularly, allows us to connect with Universal Intelligence, which is believed to be revealed through numerous methodologies: (1) universal appeal to display unique characteristics and power (2) through manifestation of Will to convey purpose (3) through believers, who also express Universal Intelligence.

I encourage each soul to seek truth that is greater than themselves.

"As we soar throughout the times, we're able to witness pictorial images both in nature and in morals. In looking into the history of man and of nations, we behold a vast and complicated machinery in continued motion; and the more we look into it, the more wonderful do we find it in all its parts. Its movements are beyond our comprehension. Who made it? Why was it made? Is it left to regulate itself? Suppose we were looking at an immense piece of mechanism, made with admirable finish; its parts fitting together, and moving with a velocity and a power which, if uncontrolled, would carry destruction to itself and to everything near it. Could we believe it made itself? Could we believe that it moved without having power communicated to it? Could we believe that the Maker had no purpose in view when he made it? Let us endeavor, then, in studying the history of the world, to learn why it was made; for we have a personal interest in knowing why. (Schieffelin, 2)

Reflection:

A.) Name five blessings you received that wasn't the result of anything you had done (personally) to receive such blessings.

1.

2.

3.

4.

5.

B.) Have you ever opened a biblical text to inquire of Universal Intelligence? Circle your answer.

Yes

No

If not, why? Please write your answer.

C.) How do you envision life without the caring aspects of Divine inspiration? Write your response.

D.) At this present moment in time, do you feel it's necessary to exert more focus on finding balance, peace and tranquility? Write your response.

E.) List five prayer requests.

1.

2.

3.

4.

5.

II. PHENOMENON

Difficult Argument: Where did humans come from?

Simple Truth: For centuries scientists' have tried to discover the existence of humans. And, for some, the hypothesis indicates that human creation is a form of evolution. Biblical text, to my knowledge, does not discuss the subject of evolution. It does, in fact, conflict with the worldview that starts without a creator. According to prophecy, man was made in the image of God.

As human beings, we seek to understand the natural wonder and era about ourselves, the cosmos of our musings that exist one starry night. As we thrive to relate to such unknown universe, we are faced with questioning ourselves. Who am I? Where did I come from? Issues relating to the origins of mankind have engaged thinkers with new urgency ever since the age of science.

We use religion in our attempt to feel more secure through our beliefs. As we study various religions, ideas are brought about from ethnic rituals learned through our society. Most religion has a sacred book that worships a divine being according its set commandments. Linguistic clues of such derivation, if correct, suggests the joining of our natural human world to that of the sacred. Our stories being expressed helps us gain understanding through development of central myths. I suppose such vision having been revealed from a supernatural realm link us all to be one through sacred guideline, and to experience emotional characteristics. Our emotions associate us with having feelings of mystery, and to experience a revelation and gain comprehension about the wedded bliss to know ecstasy. The prophetic orientation implies that a human being may be an important intermediary between the believer and the sacred. Our dreadfulness, or lack of knowledge is what sparks our conversation to praise and worship God through devotion to become liberated. Therefore, gaining clarity about Universal Intelligence makes it the only way possible to experience inner peace.

In our attempt to know God, we begin to learn more about who we are, what we're capable of and our existence. We utilize artifacts to benefit our beliefs.

Human key role is a distinction between what is considered sacred and ordinary. This, of course, is often a concern because of emphasized differentiations between the deepest levels of reality, and the mysterious originating holiness that is called many names. As a result, we seek union with a reality much greater than ourselves.

In regards to human existence, there is simply no need to render hypothesis on the occurrence of phenomena. What good does it anyhow? We should focus on things that are good and worthy of praise, things that are true, honorable, right, pure, beautiful, and respected. *Philippians 4:8*

When we confine our thoughts on things we cannot control, we end up worried, stressed, exalted, overwhelmed, or with anxiety. Why not preserve our energy to serve a much greater purpose? I'm not excluding the fact people can be curious and show interest, because without scientific experimentation technology would not have advanced as far as it has today. What's important to note is that we're incapable of giving ourselves ability, and mustn't disassociate our thoughts from the source that enables us.

Biblical text suggests that humans were created by Omnipotent energy. Argue if you must, but humans will never gain resolution on human derivation, other than the knowledge proposed to us through faith and belief.

* * *

What's important to note is that we're incapable of giving Ourselves ability, and mustn't disassociate our thoughts from the source that enables us.

* * *

It is understandable divine plans are a mystery to us, and whatever occurred was planned long ago. Everyone knows what people are like. No one can argue with a cosmic divine that is superior in every form.

Theological affirmations express that the world and everything within is not a product of blind chance and probability; things were established with a purpose by Omnipotent energy.

What set humans apart from any other animal species are (1) It is believed that we are made in God's image (2) we possess an imagination, are morally responsible and held accountable for our actions. All facets are thought to connect us with Universal Intelligence.

Humans can be awful creatures when there is no spiritual connection. As we possess learned traits of caring characteristics, we are able to ration with sympathy while also be empathic.

Scientific research supports the splendid and majestic reality of creation. True science is conducted through observation, which in terms means that theories are secondary to actual evidence.

I'm suggesting we adopt a loyal mindset, and recognize our obligation to know God, if we're to have an identity.

Reflection:

A.) Do you believe an Omnipotent source of energy is responsible for human existence? Circle your answer.

Yes

No

If no, please explain.

B.) Do you believe science supports/ and or proves God's word to be true? Explain your answer.

Yes

No

If no, please explain.

C.) How do you rate yourself? Circle your answer.

1 - Someone of little faith (struggling with faith but desire stronger connection with Divinity)

2 - Someone with faith but (less depended upon Deity for answers)

3 - Someone of great faith (depend heavily upon Deity for answers)

D.) List five challenges that prevent you from living the life you hope to live?

1.

2.

3.

4.

5.

E.) Name at least five changes you will make, in hopes of being a better person for Goodness' sake?

1.

2.

3.

4.

5.

III. SACRED WRITINGS

Difficult Argument: Humans are bound to Scripture for our knowledge from God.

Simple Truth: Biblical texts reveals God purpose for the human race. The source was transcribed as something unchangeable to man. The Bible upholds moral standards embraced by God as the foundation. These ethical standards supersede the highest moral standards known to mankind.

Biblical text asserts, *"In the beginning was the Word, and the Word was with God, and the Word was God"* John 1:1 *"All Scripture is given by inspiration of God, and is profitable for doctrine, for reproof, for correction, for instruction in righteousness, that the man of God may be complete, and thoroughly equipped for every good work."* 2 Timothy 3: 16-17

There are many concerns nowadays, and enough frustration to make anyone lose their mind. In life we are forwarded many miseries. *"Look among the nations and watch- Be utterly astounded!*

For, I will work a work in your days which you will not believe, though you were told." Habakkuk 1:5

It deems profound that biblical principles provide food for our thoughts, and perceptual insights into the needs and tensions of our time. Isn't it astounding those stories told centuries ago throughout biblical history still relates to us now in modern times? Just as sometimes we experience moments of happiness, we experience moments of sadness. There is no way we could feel good all the time. Despite whatever we should experience, or how terrible something seems, one may find comfort and assurance in the covenant of the Divine. Anyone who strives purposely to be a great Stuart of loving directives will also agree.

Scripture communicates to us those tragic moments in life that are unavoidable, and that the world will not get any better but get worse. If any person thinks that he or she can make the world a better place, they are wrong. The Noble covenant is significant to our well-being and way of life.

We can't survive spiritually without regularly renewing our love and loyalty for the Divine. Godly expression helps us to remember that Universal Intelligence is at the center of our life. We must first recognize Deity, in order to understand the desires of us.

As we partake in the characteristics of godly behavior, we then receive an eternal joy, feelings of self-worth, and essentialness to the sharing of majestic expression. Our hearts and minds are all we have against negative odds.

The reason we are bound to scripture for our knowledge from God is because we are not self-reliant. Sometimes, we share matters with those we feel are capable of helping us out of our dilemmas. Truth is, we do not always have the necessary resources to help one another, or simply choose not to. Sometimes, we consider going to a thought-to-be friend - wrong person. We seek psychiatric guidance, or pursue sleep (medication) in a bottle - wrong choice. Why? Because, spiritual enlightenment is the only thing that can render us peace of mind.

*   *   *

The reason we are bound to scripture for our knowledge from God is because we are not self-reliant.

*   *   *

According to biblical text, a proclaimed archangel (spirit of darkness) renders us satanic tendencies which distracts us from loving principles.

Here are some ways in which deception presents itself: (1) imposes doubt so that we question matters of goodness (2) discourages us so that we focus on our problems rather than Deity (3) causes diversion and make that which seems wrong seem right (4) causes delay which forces us to put off doing something important.

Repercussions are the afflictions we experience whenever resisting spiritual guidance. Here are some examples by which we can attest: betrayal, disappointment, burden, fear, anxiety, depression, oppression, deception, exploitation, destruction, abuse, sickness, disease, and fatality.

When we rely on spiritual connection, we learn to grow in mysticism and become better equipped for the challenges that we face. Afflictions can be counteracted and conquered, once in tune with Universal Intelligence. This does not mean we are exempt from consequences, but obtain a change of heart and mind as how to effectively cope with such matters.

We can accept that the afflictions that occur today has already happened, for it is written and foretold years ago. Every experience is a test of faith. Whenever examining, we shouldn't second guess Universal Intelligence, but instead utilize any intelligence to await new opportunities.

Reflection:

A.) Name five outcomes of how you suspect life would be, if we didn't have spiritual enlightenment?

1.

2.

3.

4.

5.

B.) Please take a moment to read Bible verse *Mathew 9:13*. What message did you grasp? Please explain.

IV. EFFECTIVE COMMUNICATION

Difficult Argument: No one can deny communication with the Cosmic Divine.

Simple Truth: As our faith diminishes, no matter the religion, if any, we are not subconscious from thinking or communicating with the Universal Intelligence.

Communication is personal and a primary principle that's unavoidable. We all need and desire effective communication with Deity, in order to function properly on a day-to-day basis.

Communicating effectively means being committed. The slightest neglect of communication with God allows opportunity for enticement by temptation, which we cannot handle or refrain on our own.

Now in the 21st Century, digital developments have made communicating quicker and more efficient. Because of this, there is much concern regarding the way communication is being conveyed, such as: who are we communicating with or about? How are we communicating? And, when are we choosing to communicate, if at all?

In the world today, all the world is a stage and on camera more than ever before. E-technologies have become an integral part of our lives. We are now, as communicators and artists, on view for the world. We must understand and use the best communication practice to engage the world at large, especially those of us who believe that we are God's instruments in the world for redemptive good. We must be pleasing, inspirational and captivating to viewers. We no longer communicate to only our specific sub-cultural groups; we now communicate to the entire world. Our communication must have depth and breadth that universally appeals. Our personal and corporate appearance, communication, and performance matters in terms of our ability to captivate, engage and inspire. God-given beauty, artistry, and excellence must be evident in our communication practice, especially for us to sustain the attention of viewers for the sake of goodness. This entails effective non-verbal communication also. It is especially through our body of work that we glorify God, reflecting Divine attributes, nature and spirit.

Teaching godly love is the most effective form of communication. For those who struggle with acceptance, I pray that your heart is encouraged to seek.

One might ask, "How do you know when God intervene your life?" Truth is God allows our tragic flaws to act as communication too. When we, alone, seek to suppress our hostilities we fail. When Universal Intelligence occupies our personal space, we become inspired and our circumstances doesn't seem bad as before. In other words, our bad days make us appreciate the good ones. As we decipher and grow optimistically, it is this very moment we recognize God as being an integral part of our lives.

At a very young age my brother and I were adopted by our grandparents. We knew our biological mom, despite much of her absence. What I recall most fondly was the interest she showed in Universal Intelligence by taking my brother and me to church. By the time I became a teenager, I was then the eldest of two brothers and a sister. All of us lived with our grandparents, who were fantastic individuals - very loving and caring. As old age captured them, they became very sickly unto serious medical causes. I, then, became the only member who attended church on a regular basis. Before graduating high school, both my grandparents had become deceased. Their deaths took its toile on me, and my relationship with God dwindled because of many unanswered questions. Therefore, I began to do what lots of teens did, and became occupied with things far less spiritually gratifying. To say the least, I grew weary of my religious image. I wasn't experiencing any illegal troubles, but I lost focus because I knew not what plans Universal Intelligence had in store for me.

Years later, and while now an adult, Deity gave me second chance to revisit the term "Faith." Universal Intelligence allowed me to experience both effective and non-effective forms of communication. This, of course, meant experiencing hurt and shame to learn of what was missing. As complicated as it sounds, trying times helped to appreciate the better moments. Moreover, reestablishing and maintaining a relationship with God has made the difference.

One of the greatest blessings is that moral deficit is personal related, meaning we aren't limited in our communication practice with Universal Intelligence, despite societal disconnects. It appears, nowadays, that on a massive scale people throughout society have no objections of excluding God from conversation. This is very troublesome to me. Who, then, are we receiving directives?

Communication, sometimes, deserves privacy. Through meditation/ and or communion, we seek authority of Universal Intelligence to lead us instead of us pretending we are Cosmic Divine.

In the world today technology and all of its efficiency has virtually established disconnect amongst people. Misconstrued messages take on a different meaning. Personal invitation lacks 'personal' attachment of human connection and interactive substance. Furthermore, cyber-attacks/ and or bullying through cloud-based mechanisms causes personal breach of safety undermining wireless fidelity, if there is such reliability?

Nowadays, there is an anti-humanistic drive that devalues the social and mortal aspects of our being. The enhanced robotic fusion is on full display. Thinking for ourselves has been minimized, whereas, should there be a short circuit with technology we'd all be lost in defeat unto technical glitch.

CEO's, some of the most prominent figures of tech-giant conglomerates, denote that the direction for which technology is advancing it's too late to abort from mechanized innovations. Unquestionable, we can appreciate the intuitiveness of human intelligence; however, minimal thought is considered about the effects of a personified breach. The new normalcy be that we are subject to addictions of the robotic experience.

As we travel the path of millennials, the application of scientific knowledge and social engineering only expands with time. What doesn't carry forward are the social aspects that we need as people to feel inclusive and loved.

Humans are given five traditional senses: sight, hearing, taste, smell, and touch. Despite each sensitivity having a more in-depth analysis or classification scientifically, each sense constitutes a meaningful projector, based upon previous learned information when operating face-to-face.

The less we consider these personal attributes the more out-of-touch we become to communicate 'socially' effective. It is necessary that we acquire moral sensitivity as we mature in relationship with the Divine.

V. DIPLOMAT

Difficult Argument: Have politics become the new belief system?

Simple Truth: If we do not share in the principalities of the Divine, who else can we trust and believe. *"Finally, brethren, whatever things are true, whatever things are noble, whatever things are just, whatever things are pure, whatever things are lovely, whatever things are of good report, if there is any virtue and if there is anything praiseworthy- meditate on these things. The things which you learned and received and heard and saw in me, these do, and the God of peace will be with you." Philippians 4:9*

We live in a nation where honest opinions have accepted a fictitious deception based upon radical views and man's determination to supremacy. Ethical obligation, it seems, has been replaced by selfish traits that flourish according to pursuit. At what point are we going to take accountability for our own engagements? It's the choices we often make which construct our pathways and our beliefs.

Church enthusiast, today, seem far too passionate about embracing worldly ideas. Since this appears so, who might lead the way for any credible susceptible guidance?

"Trust in the Lord with all your heart and lean not on your own understanding; in all your ways acknowledge him, and he will make your paths straight." Proverbs 3:5-6

A socialist would claim that our thinking has adopted the capitalist ideology. One does not have to be a politician to notice this world is headed for disaster. Greed seems to always bring about pessimism. It's not until bad decisions have been made, we demand an understanding of the hidden agenda behind the matter.

Self-centered notions have us tripping over our own shoe strings. Does anyone care of anything anymore?

Although, political agenda does have relevance, conversely, when misused it creates an avalanche for us all. Politics is designed to help maintain social order; yet, governmental structure, it seems, is fixated on power for one's own sake. It doesn't matter our roles in the political arena, we're all viewed the same in the eyes of the Divine.

Much of the news today is simply gossip without constructive meaning. Character, along with qualification, it seems, has taken a back seat in comparison to popularity.

The Lord tells us…

"I will bring the blind by a way they did not know; I will lead them in paths they have not known. I will make darkness light before them, and crooked places straight. These things I will do for them, and not forsake them." Isaiah 42:16

Historically, political ascendancy has had a dramatic decline in its ability to maintain good characterization. Throughout the intervening years, man fall from grace presents himself more now than ever before. Those who walk a path without spiritual insight are easily deceived and gullible targets. They are captured in the mainstream media; whereas, gossip becomes their new god.

* * *

Those who walk a path without spiritual insight are easily deceived and gullible targets.

* * *

Traditionally, politics and money go hand and hand. But they who base their class at the core of their hearts seem to have forgotten that status doesn't bring forth peace of mind. In fact, human downfall is caused by characteristic flaw. We reach a premise that our lives have been built upon, and reluctantly refuse to acknowledge right from wrong. Moral values are an upmost concern. At great levels of responsibility, we prefer candidates to possess a wise ego, despite immature decisions being made at prestige levels.

We debate the role of elected officials, but indoctrination should include one's spiritual acceptance for the love of the Divine. If this isn't so, at what point did we lose sight of dignity?

People are denying that their own wickedness is the cause of their own agony. This trend has now drifted into the world of politics. Unfortunately, the human predicament and forms of other foolish escapisms are supported by worldly psychology. However, we've got to do better with policing up ourselves. The way for this to happen is by engaging Universal Intelligence at the forefront of our lives. Accumulatively, we would function better as a whole.

"Be hospitable to one another without grumbling. As each one has received a gift, minister it to one another as good stewards of the manifold grace of God." 1Peter 4:9-10

"Remove the reality of sin, and you take away the possibility of repentance. Abolish the doctrine of human depravity and you void the divine plan of salvation. Erase the notion of personal guilt and you eliminate the need for a Savior. Obliterate the human conscience, and you will raise an amoral and unredeemable generation. The church cannot join hands with the world in such a grossly satanic enterprise. To do so is to overthrow the very gospel we are called to proclaim" MacArthur, Jr.

Reflection:

A.) Do you feel that spiritual guidance is a necessary asset to be an effective leader? Circle your answer.

Yes

No

If no, please explain.

B.) Do you think the political spectrum is run like a cult? Circle your answer.

Yes

No

If no, please explain.

C.) There is nothing wrong with fulfilling the role of a politician; however, do you feel that God should be at the forefront of decisions being made? Circle your answer.

Yes

No

D.) To conduct the job of a politician do you think there is ever a point where church and state are inseparable?

Yes

No

If no, please write your response.

E.) Considering Omnipotent energy is responsible for our ability, is it morally sound to be successful without giving God glory for the accomplishments?

Yes

No

If yes, please write your response.

VI. REALITY VERSUS PLEASURE PRINCIPLE

Difficult Argument: Which is more important... a commodity, or the ideology behind its creation?

Simple Truth: Every human is created for great purpose. Unlike those things we shall never understand, our ultimate goal is to stimuli humanity with Divine purpose.

I'm convinced that many people operate in a real unconscious state of mind. With much concern, thinking rationally appears odd, due to individual behavior directed toward immediate gratification.

We have become psychologically scorned from materialism. Our political, economic, and social opinions are being determined according to self-motives. Reasonability has been deferred to instant gratification because of immatureness. In whole, people lack understanding of moral character based on unreasonable practices.

Being popular with status at a very young age seems to be the new modern adaptation, ignoring the fact that erotic gratification interrupts personality development. Nowadays, many have lost touch with character dispositioning themselves to things like fetishism, which creates an alienated world making individuals feel non-existing.

Truth is, when we are stripped of our belongings, we result back to the reality of things. The so-called "Recession" is a prime example. For many people, a recession forced them to re-adjust their mindsets, or to focus on that which truly matters. The ideal summation is a higher calling.

The pleasure principle defines one as being arrogant, greedy, selfish, and untrustworthy. What's even more disturbing is the concept of being naïve. *"They do not know it, but they are doing it. The very concept of ideology implies a kind of basic, constitutive naiveté: the misrecognition of its own presuppositions, of its own effective conditions, a distance, a divergence between so-called social reality and our distorted representation, our false consciousness of it" (Literary 717).*

When considering the pleasure principle, the issue exists when we think too highly of ourselves. We tend to forget Universal Intelligence is greater than anything and everything. We allow our status quo, or material fortunes to represent us when these things aren't worth any value.

Something to ponder: Universal Intelligence is responsible for all creation. Currency is replicated by humans. Humans develop superstructures, as well as, the items contrary to that human need generating arbitrary numbers that it takes to produce or buy products. An unfair use-exchange value becomes the focus of the superstructure creating a sub-culture. This method places humans in a false consciousness, an illusion of human activity and attachment. Human sense obligations to sponsor these attachments, while, forget the Cosmic Divine is the supplier of our every need.

Long story short, we spend far too much time being concerned with nonsense. Certainly, it's pleasant to have and afford nice things; but our egos are embedded and manifested into thinking materialistically. We fail to give Deity admiration for our gain, while act with distorted minds as if responsible for our own achievements. We're not!

It is vital we understand that the conscious is informed by tradition, as well as by truth; so, the standards it holds us to are not necessarily theological. The conscience can be needlessly condemning in areas where there is no biblical issue, yet attempt to stronghold us from Universal Intelligence. Circumstances unparallel to our true calling in life.

As a testament of Universal Intelligence, the (reality principle), in the case of a recession, many people less fortunate (financially) were grateful for peace of mind.

According to the U.S. News World Report online, despite lingering unemployment and a still sluggish economy, many Americans find reasons to be thankful. In fact, for some, unexpected layoffs, financial setbacks, or simply a desire to spend more time with family have served as a reality check, a wake-up call for consumers to rethink their idea of wealth and prosperity. People are focusing more on life satisfaction than satisfaction by consumption. One of the big shifts is that people are questioning, 'Is the time that I'm spending bringing me greater satisfaction in my life versus something that is just on autopilot?' "More money doesn't necessarily lead to greater happiness. People are looking for ways to realign with family and the values that matter to them.

In regards to the pleasure principle, an article posted online by the Associated Press, "How much crazier can Black Friday get?" reveals the mindset of people without divine insight in their lives. Customers risk being pepper-sprayed, causing fight scenes, as well as, looting, and wonder how such events evolve? Proclaimed experts say a volatile mix of desperate retailers, cutthroat marketing, bargained-obsessed shoppers who are sleep-deprived and short tempered are responsible for the increased frenzies. They even go as far to say that online-coupon phenomenon's psychological hunger is fed for finding impossible bargains, and that these people who should know better should have enough stuff already.

It's alarming to see an awful lot of psychology were used to evaluate those encouraged or influenced by the notion of scarcity. Despite advice given from those to prevent this from happening, there is no doubt that afflictions render exposure.

Reflection:

A.) Which is more important a commodity, or the ideology behind its creation?

Please write your response.

B.) Do you think materialistic values can sustain peace of mind? If you feel that it can, please explain.

C.) Have you ever had something you greatly desired/and or obtained, but was still unhappy after receiving it? Circle your answer.

Yes

No

Please explain.

D.) Is Deity at the center of your life?

Yes

No

If no, please explain.

E.) Why would a person who is rich feel depressed and miserable?

Please write your response.

VII. OPTIMISM VERSUS PESSIMISM

Difficult Argument: Despite dilemmas, we should reference Universal Intelligence about the critical factors of all matters.

Simple Truth: Positive thinking helps to deliver us from moments that don't seem promising.

There are circumstances over which we have no control. Take heredity for instance but we can control the decisions that we make. At the heart of the matter is the sin-oriented nature we have all inherited. It can be partly controlled, although not overcome by human effort. The solution that Universal Intelligence offers is not control but a changed life. To have a changed life, trust the Divine, and begin to change your attitude toward others.

There is power in positive thinking. Surely a circumstance can be worse, but while we exist our presence alone ministers to someone else's condition.

The general personality of someone who is optimistic believes that final outcomes are positive ones. Do you not agree that positive thought is better than thinking things will turn out for the worse?

Matters in life can sometimes be difficult, but there is a mystery of Divinity within us all to overcome barriers.

What does it mean for us to think positively? How does it make us feel to sincerely wish someone else their very best? If individual thoughts are always negative, ever contemplate why? To know the root cause of our own bitterness is a vital step toward overcoming such negative attitude.

I've found that spiritual enlightenment helps to drive home the "I can" attitude and foster positivity. Motivational speeches sometimes render more personified vindications.

Let's discuss the mindset of someone who anticipates undesirable outcomes. Is it safe to assume that this person has very little faith, or are afraid that success might change their identity?

A look on a person's face sometimes can be misleading. A fictitious smile in its attempt can temporarily cover up feelings of hurt and sadness. Ultimately, pretension is false and cannot deceive a person's heart. Truth will always display what/how a person really feels.

After serving ten years in the United States Military, and having been deployed to war on several occasions, I can officially say, "Good times outweighed the bad." This wasn't always my view on life. I've learned that no problem is too great for the Celestial.

My tenure in service ended abruptly unto medical impairment. Needless to say, I wasn't prepared for transitioning back into the civilian sector. Transitioning for me meant altering my hyper-ego, and resulting to a noncombatant lifestyle. The experience was tough. I possessed more of a pessimistic view on life, and blamed past familiarizations for the toile it had on me mentally and physically. I sought counseling in the event that it would help alleviate anxiety and depression; I, therefore, agreed to partake in therapeutic group sessions. It was a defining moment. I knew it was vital for me to transition from pessimism to adopting a more optimized perspective. I, therefore, made the decision to dedicate my time gaining spiritual enlightenment. Eventually and overtime, my heart exceeded contention with hope that everything was fine. Ever since, it has been my desire to help inspire and encourage those in need.

One of the things that I've been fortunate to do is work with youth. To the extent, my involvement extends within communities, juvenile detention centers, state and alternative schools. I denote that many afflictions that occur with youth are very harsh, yet extensive. The root cause of these conditions is certainly a lack of love, care and trust. My approach has been pragmatic. Unless they can trust me, they'll never commit to the sincerity I hope to share.

Trust requires loyalty and commitment. It is true that we never know how we might respond to predicaments unless placed in situations. It is best we keep an open-mindset to know there is always an alternative. I consider this approach 'Alternative Reasoning.'

Pessimistic views blot alternative perspectives. Nevertheless, it is beneficial to contrast negative situations in order to derive at a much more meaningful outcome.

VIII.
PROFOUND REFLECTIONS

Difficult Argument: Biblical history gives rise to the human condition.

Simple Truth: As humans we often operate and maneuver throughout life without fully understanding who we are as people, or what our purpose is. Universal Intelligence confronts us with history that are too difficult to ignore. It also references afflictions that occur today. Even though Biblical principles and teachings are labeled methodical, it has a tendency to sway truth because of foretold information that attests modern circumstances. And, since we are only human through each other, its sacred guidelines are established so that we might know how to live a righteous life.

Coming to grip with foretold information can be baffling to us, especially when it brings to fruition that we acknowledge and have learned.

The Bible is a resource used to commemorate with a higher power, and to draw connecting knowledge about modern instances. As we seek to understand the present, without working knowledge of the past history would surely repeat itself. We look to the past for mannerism and for ways to cope with errors. One might ask, "How, then, does biblical history give rise to the human condition?" Perhaps, it's best to shed light on the term "History." History possesses a broad spectrum, and is commonly used to reference past events and times associated with the human race. The chronological account involves concepts which embrace social, political, and religious perspectives.

Biblical history entails profound bibliography. Historians pursue a philosophical approach that includes comprehensive implications, essentially, archeological evidence and the search for the Celestial, in order to understand mankind. Scholars find themselves heavily involved with exploration of ancient Middle Eastern kingdoms. Their finding of artifacts renders notions about the general cultural, social, and international circumstances that took place during biblical times. Biblical text reserves trustworthy data that produces historical memory, and is somehow relevant for understanding that history. Historical claims that minister to the human conditions force recognition and our attention on that which matters most, love.

Critics have their opinions. However, Biblical history offers us a narrative account of people and events that extends from creation to the end of the Judean Empire, and events in Jerusalem that took place under Persian law. It also provides a host of prophetic books that allude to national and international conditions, and exiles that occurred after ruling in the Babylonian courts. The Bible reports of great empires being organized strategically. Moreover, it teaches us about the gospel narratives of agony, and presumes a graphic view of world history through exposure.

If we don't believe in something, we'll fall for anything!

Biblical texts render suspected notions about how human society functions, what patterns of change tend to occur, and under what circumstances. It alludes to human history being guided by divine intervention.

Biblical accuracy will always be questioned, even though theologians have drawn much attention to historical matters throughout the years. Regardless of the philosophy behind one's practice, it is difficult to ignore the concepts from which the ancient data emerged.

Since the beginning of an unknown timeframe, the Bible conveys there to be evil in the world since the creation of humans. In fact, this evil nature is detrimental to us all in the present time.

According to prophecy of there being an end time for us all, aside from historical evidence or any archeological findings, the Bible as history details significant implications that test our fate.

Reflection:

A.) Do you agree or disagree that Biblical history gives rise to the human condition? Please circle your answer.

Agree

Disagree

If you agree please explain how? If you disagree, please explain why?

B.) Do you feel that the Bible is a profound reflection of things that is to occur in our present time? Circle your answer.

If no, please explain.

C.) Events that have occurred throughout Bible history is enough to draw query and label the book as the most important book ever written? Circle your answer.

Yes

No

If no, please explain.

D.) List five things that are most interested about the Bible?

1)

2)

3)

4)

5)

IX. MORAL DISCREPANCY '*THE GRIEVING CONSCIENCE*'

Difficult Argument: The human conscience, instinctively, cause us to examine ourselves.

Simple Truth: We're mystified by our inadequate nature, deficiencies, and incapacity to do everything accurate. Both the mind and conscience can become so tarnished that they dismiss making discrepancy between what is pure and contaminated. Yet, the Omnipotent designed the conscience with the ability to sense right from wrong. This explains why humans result to alternative satisfying methods so that we may think more greatly of ourselves.

As people, logic tells us when we are traversing away from the presence of the higher calling. Perception makes us aware of the contradiction between thought and action. John MacArthur Jr. asserts, "The danger of irregularity between thought and unattractive behavior is the threat of generating a lifelong memoir that would stalk our apologetic integrity having to offer a lifespan confession for our faults."

If remorse is not earnest our integrity would drown in denial.

A refined smart conscience signals us of ethical standards before we act, making us responsible or feel frightened of future punishment, if we disobey its limitations.

The thought process of an evil being is confusion. The wicked spirit of that being is dishonesty. Unresolved guilt is a true burden of a misleading conscience that is hindered by conceit and indulgence. The result of such destructive engagements is that which causes us to mourn from past actions in the present.

Instinctively, we all desire to be better people. And, since we are incapable of sustaining good motives on our own, we deviate in hopes to discover answers so our lives can be healthier.

Everyone knows that there are penalties for every action taken. Otherwise, why do things if we don't expect to get results?

What we do can establish a series of proceedings that may endure long after we are extinct. Regrettably, when we make choices, most of us think of instant gratifications. These are often deceptive because they are brief. Perhaps, we don't know the lasting effects of most judgments we make. This fact alone should cause us to think more wisely, and pursue Divine directive as we make choices in life.

In order for the conscience to function in accordance with true sacredness, it must be educated by spiritual enlightenment. When remorseful spirits are without a loving foundation, this is a sign of anguish and the need for spiritual growth, in order to be in synchronization with the Celestial Divine. And, because the conscience reacts to persuasions of the mind, it can be stimulated and honed by spiritual implications.

As people it is our obligation to safeguard our integrity. In fact, it's the most perplexing duty. Although the conscience pleads us to do what we trust is right, it detains us from doing what we consider dishonest. The conscience, alone, is a temporal faculty that judges our engagements and beliefs by way of the highest standards we perceive. So, then, as we infringe upon our thoughts, it convicts us, proposing moods of humiliation, grief, repentance, concern, degradation, or even anxiety. When we follow our conscience, it applauds us, bringing happiness, tranquility, comfort, and dignity to fruition.

The conscience knows our central motivation and true beliefs. It is beyond motive and understanding. We can try justifying in our own minds, but the conscience cannot be easily persuaded. The conscience is sensitive by tradition, as well as by fact, so the values it holds us to are not automatically scriptural. It can hold us to the very thing the Noble is trying to release us from, similar in comparison to that of an addiction. The conscience is privy to secret thoughts and motives being more precise as a stern observer.

A frail conscience may result from being uninformed by spiritual enlightenment, or by possessing weak faith not yet deterred from worldly sways. To overcome such pathetic gesture, admit and abandon recognized evil, scrutinize your faults in light of righteousness, and educate the conscience by focusing on trustworthy facts that correlates to pleasingly discovered realities.

X. DICHOTOMY - *MIND OR MATTER*

Difficult Argument: We can do anything that we focus our minds on.

Simple Truth: The division of thought and belief contradicts, according to actions. – Terrance B. McGee

How often do we know of the correct thing to do but do the opposite? Have you ever asked yourself why? Truth is *"The distinction between mind and body is an artificial dichotomy, a discrimination which is unquestionably based far more on the peculiarity of intellectual understanding than on the nature of things." Carl Jung*

We are resources to be used for greater purposes in life. A widely used phrase or cliché is that "I am only human." Although such statement is thought provoking, we also possess God-like characteristics, and can do much when focused with the belief that we're capable.

It's always easier to talk a great spill than it is to follow through and complete obligations. Instinctively, we all desire to be better people. And, since we are incapable of sustaining good motives on our own, we digress in hope to find solutions so our lives can be better. *"A time of crisis is not just a time of anxiety and worry. It gives a chance, an opportunity, to choose well or to choose badly." Desmond Tutu*

The underline premise of thought is that the focus tends to sway and choose accordingly that which has precedence over us. Fortunately, positive thought, for heaven's sake, does not align with negative actions or that which consumes us in terms of worse.

*   *   *

The underline premise of thought is that the focus tends to sway and choose accordingly that which has precedence over us.

*   *   *

Moral victory is to overcome a bearing. It is the intestinal fortitude (will power) that one possesses to help obtain a desired goal. It's never the matter itself, but how we see and think about things. To foresee matters as being unfair means resisting positive aspects, and accepting horrible conditions making the self out to be a victim.

The ideal goal of defeating pessimistic views on life is to entertain the possibility of there being more than one way to view occurrences. Since we cannot control things that happen to us, it is imperative we understand that we can control our own happiness, or lack of it.

Pain is inevitable, but suffering is optional. Because we are not exempt to falling victim to circumstance, when trouble impedes it is ONLY a fraction of our psychological struggle. Therefore, as the mind is strengthened, we are afforded a sense of power that can unlock unlimited progression. We must be smarter in our decision-making approach.

In high school, I was considered one of the most valuable basketball players all four years of attendance. Basketball appeared a lifeline. I was contingent upon gaining a scholarship to attend one of the better colleges. I had no clue this would be derailed by fuzzy decision making. I fail to capitalize on scholarships that were afforded me. Moreover, I missed out on a potential life changing invitation, a chance to participate in the McDonald's All American Basketball Classics.

A year had past, and I had yet to establish any solid plans for my future. After numerous failed attempts, I decided to enlist into the United States Military.

After three years of service, I received replacement orders overseas to Germany. Despite mission-oriented tasks, whenever the time was permissible, I played basketball against numerous leagues throughout the country. This lifetime opportunity afforded me recognition and the chance to play ball professionally. Although a dream come true, I had to decide on what was best to support me and my family. So, I refrained from pursuing a basketball career, and instead chose to remain in military service, which deemed fundamentally more secure.

By 2004, my family and I were back stateside in California. It didn't take long before getting recognized on the court again. I was scouted by a sports director at a recreational facility, who admired my skillset and felt I had what it took to play ball professionally with the Army League. I gladly accepted the invitation and headed out to the Rocky Mountains in Colorado.

In a three weeks timespan, I had gotten seriously injured. The injury forfeited my chances of making the team; therefore, I could no longer play and was sent back to my assigned duty placement. It seemed that from that moment matters continued in a downward spiral.

Months following, while on a reconnaissance mission, I became seriously injured a second time in a tactical vehicle rollover. The injuries sustained led to medical impairment. To say the least, my career ended abrupt. Nothing in life seemed fair at that point. I pondered many questions such as, "Where do I go from here? Why was this happening to me? Who can I turn to for advice about my issues?"

For ten years, being a military soldier was my life. It was what I knew. To suddenly conclude without warning was mind boggling. Transition was harsh. Needless to say, I felt like a prisoner locked away in some unknown dimension. Antisocial impediments of depression and anxiety were in full effect. Over time, I was able to identify past strongholds, deficits and misplacement.

I understand my injury as redirection to a new course in life. The old self, both naïve and immature, would've obscured this happiness thinking I knew what was best for me. I'm not saying that I applaud being injured, but had I continued down the same old path I might've been consumed by other worldly deceits.

I've learned that <u>ONLY</u> we can allow ourselves to remain prisoner of the mind. We cannot lose dignity unless we personally relinquish it.

A healthy recovery mechanism has been to acknowledge my ailments/ and or condition, and to experiment with new ways of improving the circumstances.

Vicious cycles in life will forever continue and are detrimental to our health when we cling to entrapment as victims. Procrastination to take a stance against the struggles that we face isn't a healthy solution. Way to often people criticize the way matters are versus reversing criticism to foresee what obligations we have in the matter.

Each person is an authority upon their own life. My suggestion is to shift your paradigm, and be open to the possibility of new opportunities that you might not grasp should you not alter your mindset.

XI. CODE OF ETHICS – "ARISING INFLUENCE"

Difficult Argument: *If we do not stand for something, we will fall for anything!*

Simple Truth: *The Lord is a sure foundation for our times, a rich store of salvation, wisdom and knowledge. Isaiah 33:6*

Do you know who you are from God's observation? People frequently pursue an identity with limited knowledge about Universal Intelligence. Despite our ignorance, Deity reminds us repetitively.

Ever consider how moral values play an integral role in our spiritual connection with God? Everyone has needs and aspirations. Unless we discover those ambitions, our lives will appear empty, worthless and unfulfilling.

Moral values are principles that each of us abide. Consequently, what we learn is often displayed outwardly through our actions. Knowledge is obtained from both a directional and in-directional stance. Either influence can be hazardous to our well-being, if the receiver isn't educated on a righteous way of living.

Honorable standards depict our connection with the Cosmic Divine. Hence, when we aren't living according to spiritual enlightenment, our characteristic flaws are exposed.

If Universal Intelligence declares a sure foundation for our times, a rich store of salvation, wisdom and knowledge; we don't have to suffer any lack, sell our soul, or lose our identity based upon unreasonable practices.

Code of ethic fosters moral responsibilities. We have a due diligence to be great stewards, and to care for one another using loving principles as our foundation. Moral sensibilities depict where we are with Universal Intelligence.

Ethical standards are not a reflection of greed or selfishness. Theological doctrine speaks candidly about decrease of prosperity, misconstruction, and mishandling of Divine expression to fixate ungodly practices. As we develop an obsession over materialism, we become vulnerable targets to fiction away from pleasing the Highest Authority.

One of the things that I've been able to acknowledge is child innocence. Since birth, we have a need to be loved and cared for. This is factual, due to children not being able to obtain certain things on our own.

As a child grows older, the way he or she responds is predicated upon the teachings they've learned. There are appropriate times to learn of specific things. To become fully aware of certain exposures before it's time interferes with the personality development of the child.

Children are naïve about the effects of materialism. And, despite their differences, it doesn't matter if they're fortunate, less fortunate, black, white, Hispanic, or otherwise socially. Trouble impedes <u>after</u> knowledge of ownership. And, not that it's a terrible thing to own something, characteristic flaw of self-endangerment lives within obsession or fascination.

As a person gets wrapped into worldly fixations, this person must also do what it takes to uphold the addiction. It is understandable that many people are born into unusual situations that causes them to become exposed to things prematurely; yet, to accept one's character, based upon his or her negative predicament undermines the power and the ability to think and be different.

A popular cliché is that life is what we make of it. Scriptural doctrine conveys to us that a successful life has already been ordained for us; however, we can choose to negate that success by way of permitting stubbornness or rejection.

To each is own the idea of success. For some, success may be simple as overcoming simple tasks or obstacles, while for others success may be obtaining wealth or becoming rich financially, gaining spiritual inclination, or all of the above.

According to theological teachings, the art of success is wisdom. Wisdom is based upon spiritual principles of unconditional love shared through applied application. To love the self begins with indoctrination to serve with a gracious spirit.

The ideology encompassing finding an identity is to diligently and persistently strive to maintain the embodiment of sanity and positive progression. This can only be done by virtue of a genuine collaborative effort to help educate the self.

The first step is to apply proper mind etiquette. This method consists of getting rid of those things that hinder us from having a clear vision of our goals in life.

Here are a few setbacks that hinder us: (1) Self-procrastination, low self-esteem, fear (2) People with negative influences (3) Consumption of worldly fixations

To gain better clarity of each stumbling block, consider the following:

(1) Self-procrastination is simply deferment, based upon misjudgment, inaccuracy, or lazy mentality. Such reluctant nature poses negligence to fulfill any tasking.

(2) People with negative influences are simply burdens. These types of people thrive on seeing others fail.

If someone in your life is a hinder of positive progression, it's worth disassociating with those individuals for the sake of accomplishments. If it seems impossible, try altering the correlation or method for which you associate with the individual(s). To wait may be too late.

(3) Consumption of worldly fixations is the biggest challenge in today's society. It is inevitable to avoid; moreover, much is broadcast globally through virtual connection. Although media is not necessarily a bad thing, when misused or consumed it causes distraction from positive progression. We **<u>MUST</u>** consider our association to it.

Understanding code of ethics implies acceptance of self to help minimize and reframe from negative peer pressure and influences. The better we understand ourselves we're far less vulnerable then knowing nothing about who we are, or what our goals are in life.

If you are someone who's experiencing confusion, I recommend setting personal lifetime goals. Goal setting is a powerful process for thinking about your ideal future, and for motivating you to turn your vision of that future into reality.

The process of setting goals helps us choose where we wish to go in life. By knowing precisely what we wish to achieve, we can know where to concentrate our efforts. Setting goals allow us to build confidence and take pride in our accomplishments. It helps us recognize our own ability and competence in achieving the goals we've set. As we began to organize our time and resources, it is then we begin the process to make the very most of our lives.

An important notation is making sure the goals we set are ones that we genuinely set out for us, and not objectives someone else prefer us to have. As top priority, it's critical we find a spiritual balance to help support our effort.

True empowerment of understanding code of ethics is possessing high moral values. This is possible through our social connection with Divinity. The applied application incorporates analytical reasoning, which in term initiates opportunity for maintaining a critical thinking balance, and compliments our understanding before we make choices.

Every person is analytical to some degree because we all make choices. However, selections are based upon what looks right to us. Therefore, in the instance there's no spiritual connection, we make decisions despite knowing a decision to be wrong. In this case, we are blindsided by the attempt to make negative selections seem right.

In the general scheme of decision making, we should ask ourselves:

- Is what I've decided to do the correct thing?

- What is the cost of the decision I am making?

- How will my decision affect me if things don't go as planned?

- Can I live with my decision, even if it negatively affects me or someone else?

- Will my decision come back to haunt me a day, week, month, or years from now?

Here are some wise motifs (Code of Ethics) that constitute a successful initiative:

- Understand & accept that we are ONLY a resource to be used purposefully.

  - *There is no higher religion than public service*

- Commit to Honesty & Self-integrity

  - *Proper decision making begins with truth and sincerity to thy self*

- Appreciate failure as a strengthening mechanism

  - *Accept your mistakes and learn from them*

  - *Except criticism as an intuitive teaching method for potential growth*

- Learn to communicate effectively

  - *Majority of people's issues can be avoided or resolved by communicating effectively*

  - *Speak positively to the self, in hopes to avoid negative thinking*

  - *Be a great listener, open to other people's opinions and ideas, and seek to render positive feedback*

- Associate with positive people

  - *Consider those individuals who have made a difference, are making a difference, striving to make a difference, and willing to make a difference*

- *Be proactive and not reactive in your decision making*

• Be appreciative and complain less

- *Be grateful for the opportunity to impact someone else's life, whether it be directly or indirectly*

"An eclectic view of the sunset rises by morning. But this is nothing new; Universal Intelligence has always been available. Yet, our shallow minds and blurred vision causes us to defer the truth. We are, therefore, impaired by self-affliction. Examine the heart and be astoundingly amazed how love infiltrates. Examine the brain and be exceedingly amazed how the conscious declares our being. We are God-like fractions of Divine existence. But our entirety is contingent upon a glorifying correspondent." - Terrance B. McGee

XII. HUMAN NATURE

Difficult Argument: Since the beginning of an unknown time-frame, the Bible conveys there to be evil in the world since the creation of humans.

Simple Truth: The contradictions and absurdities of the human spirit could best be borne by stance of ironic detachment from the Cosmic Divine. Something that seems small or trivial to us can actually impact heavily and negatively, if we are not properly rooted.

We must, first, understand our own wickedness before we can begin to deal with it. According to biblical assertion, sin is categorized as any thought, or act against the law of God, and applies to everyone.

What I find most interesting is that those who say they don't believe in God are able to perceive distinction of the terms good and evil. Derivation of the term good is best described from scriptural teachings.

When we humble ourselves, we're more inclined to accept learned strategies for coping and dealing with matters. Without Divine sovereignty, coping or handling wickedness is not attainable.

Wickedness is inevitable. Universal Intelligence justifies the ridiculous through faith. Anyone who thinks indifferent mind is certainly discombobulated. As we seek to infiltrate the heart of human nature, what is this instinctual drive that makes us think we can handle evil on our own? We can't! Whatever it is about the wildlife of iniquity, gives rise to the wonders of infatuation or addiction.

I will not hesitate to admit having done some shameful things in my past. What I recall most fondly was having the choice to choose differently. We're all given options to make decisions; hence, the results of those decisions bring forth specific self-inflictions.

Inheritance or indoctrination to worldly fixations contributes largely to evil nature. The world view of iniquity is equated with obsession or addiction, while, biblical teaching teaches that too much of anything is a sin. Consequently, this projects that depending on consumption depicts what's considered evil and what's not. However, to try and reference wickedness is to speak in a broad spectrum. To each their own understanding; however, the detailed implications of the message does not defer from lovingness.

There will always be a debate on the subject of Theology. Question is, what do you believe? Who do you believe? How do you think and feel on the subject matter? Why is it concerning what others think?

You have a right to the journey that you're traveling. In conclusion, "the biggest distraction is the one we give ourselves." – Terrance B. McGee

References

- Henry David Thoreau, "Walden," 1854 | Introduction to Literature

- "A time of crisis is not just a tie of anxiety and worry. It gives a chance, an apology, to choose well or to choose badly." - Desmond Tutu

- "The distinction between mind and body is an artificial dichotomy, a discrimination which is unquestionably based far more on the peculiarity of intellectual understanding than on the nature of things." - Carl Jung

- Difficult Arguments and Simple Truths exploits prejudice with arguments that are debatable. In a timespan called life, *"The strength of what we believe is measured by how much we are willing to suffer those beliefs."* – Terrance B. McGee

As human beings, our limited foresight about where we derive leaves us in awe with limited knowledge about Universal Intelligence. Our different sectors and learned traditions be partly the reason for discombobulation.

The simple truths are pragmatic opinions and extracts of learned information and experiences. Although humans are challenged to remain conscious, modern day afflictions advance exposures of our conditions and daily practices for living.